HOW TO DRAW KNIGHTS AND CASTLES

SALARIYA

Published in Great Britain in MMXII by
Book House, an imprint of
The Salariya Book Company Ltd
25 Marlborough Place, Brighton BN1 1UB

3 5 7 9 8 6 4 2 1

Please visit our website at **www.salariya.com**
for **free** electronic versions of:
You Wouldn't Want to Be an Egyptian Mummy!
You Wouldn't Want to Be a Roman Gladiator!
You Wouldn't Want to Be a Polar Explorer!
**You Wouldn't Want to Sail on a 19th-Century
    Whaling Ship!**

Author: Mark Bergin was born in Hastings in 1961.
He studied at Eastbourne College of Art and has
specialised in historical reconstructions as well as
aviation and maritime subjects since 1983. He lives
in Bexhill-on-Sea with his wife and three children.

Editor: Victoria England

PB ISBN: 978-1-907184-67-3

A CIP catalogue record for this
book is available from the
British Library.

Printed and bound in China.
Printed on paper from
sustainable sources.

**WARNING: Fixatives should be
used only under adult supervision.**

Visit our websites to read interactive
free web books, stay up to date with
new releases, catch up with us on
the Book House Blog, view our
electronic catalogue and more!

www.book-house.co.uk
Information books
and graphic novels

www.scribobooks.com
Fiction books

www.scribblersbooks.com
Books for babies, toddlers and
pre-school children.

Follow us on Facebook and
Twitter by visiting
www.salariya.com

PAPER FROM
SUSTAINABLE
FORESTS

Contents

Making a start

Learning to draw is about looking and seeing. Keep practising and get to know your subject. Use a sketchbook to make quick drawings. Start by doodling and experimenting with shapes and patterns. There are many ways to draw but this book shows only some methods. Visit art galleries, look at artists' drawings and see how your friends draw, but above all, find your own way.

Practise sketching people in everyday surroundings. This will help you to draw faster and train you to capture the main elements of a pose.

Remember that practice makes perfect. If a drawing looks wrong, start again. Keep working at it — the more you draw, the more you will learn.

Perspective

If you look at any object from different viewpoints, you will see that whichever part is closest to you looks larger, and the part furthest away from you looks smaller. Drawing in perspective is a way of creating a feeling of depth — of suggesting three dimensions on a flat surface.

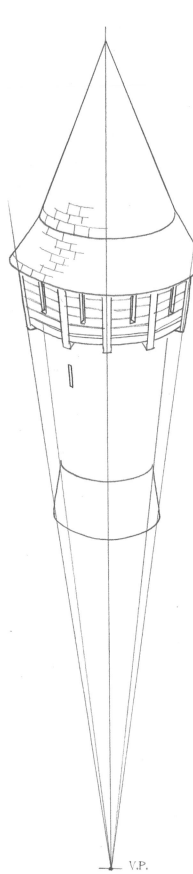

V.P.

V.P. = vanishing point

Low eye level
(view from below)

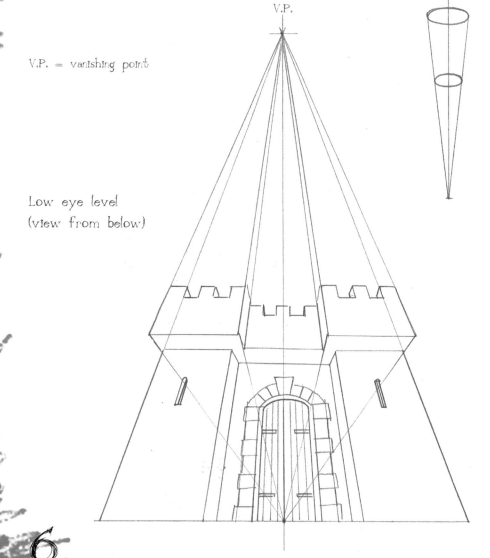

V.P.

6

Two-point perspective uses two vanishing points: one for lines running along the length of the object, and one on the opposite side for lines running across the width of the object.

Two-point perspective drawing

V.P.

V.P.

Normal eye level

Three-point perspective drawing

V.P.

V.P.

High eye level
(view from above)

V.P.

The vanishing point (V.P.) is the place in a perspective drawing where parallel lines appear to meet. The position of the vanishing point depends on the viewer's eye level. Sometimes a low viewpoint can give your drawing added drama.

7

Drawing materials

Try using different types of drawing papers and materials. Experiment with charcoal, wax crayons and pastels. All pens, from felt-tips to ballpoints, will make interesting marks — try drawing with pen and ink on wet paper for a variety of results.

Hard **pencil** leads are greyer and soft pencil leads are blacker. Hard pencils are graded from 6H (the hardest) through 5H, 4H, 3H and 2H to H. Soft pencils are graded from B, 2B, 3B, 4B and 5B up to 6B (the softest).

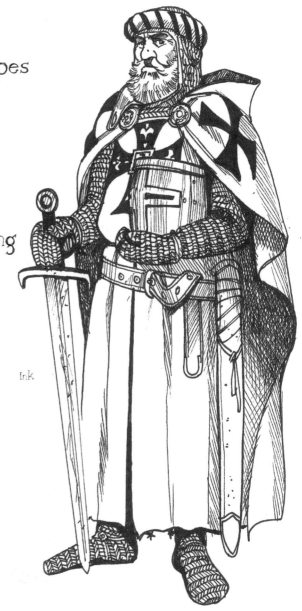

Ink

Pencil

Lines drawn in **ink** cannot be erased, so keep your ink drawings sketchy and less rigid. Don't worry about mistakes as these lines can be lost in the drawing as it develops.

Charcoal is very soft and can be used for big, bold drawings. Ask an adult to spray your charcoal drawings with fixative to prevent smudging.

Felt-tip

Ink silhouette

Pastels are even softer than charcoal, and come in a wide range of colours. Ask an adult to spray your pastel drawings with fixative to prevent smudging.

You can create special effects in a drawing done with wax crayons by scraping parts of the colour away.

Silhouette is a style of drawing that uses only a solid black shape.

9

Studies from life

Drawing from life or photographs can help you to identify shape and form. It can also develop both your drawing skills and your eye for detail.

Make a tracing of a photograph and draw a grid of squares on it.

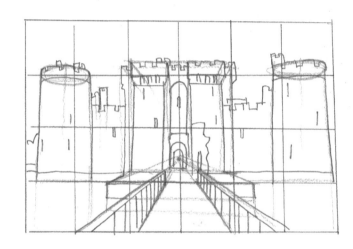

Now take a piece of drawing paper of the same proportions and draw a grid on it, either enlarging or reducing the scale of the squares' size. You can now copy shapes from each square of the tracing to the drawing paper, using the grid to guide you.

A quick sketch can often be as informative as a careful drawing that has taken many hours.

To make your drawing look three-dimensional, decide which side the light source is coming from, and put in areas of shadow where the light doesn't reach.

Sketch in an overall tone and add surrounding textures to create interest and a sense of movement. Pay attention to the position of your drawing on the paper; this is called composition.

Castle keep and towers

The keep is the central, or core, castle building. Towers were built at intervals along the castle walls to strengthen them and provide accommodation for castle workers or visitors.

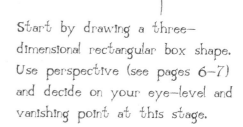

Start by drawing a three—dimensional rectangular box shape. Use perspective (see pages 6—7) and decide on your eye—level and vanishing point at this stage.

Add a tower at each corner of the keep.

You can use a ruler to make sure the initial construction lines are straight. Freehand drawing will look more interesting thereafter.

Sketch in doorways.

Draw in battlements or crenellations to the top of the castle walls and towers.

Mark in the position of the windows.

Work your way around the battlements to give them a three-dimensional effect at the top.

Draw in the tiled roofs.

Draw in the stairway and door.

Carefully draw in the stonework to make the walls look more realistic.

Add details to the stonework over all doors and windows.

Add more detail to the base of the keep walls.

Draw in the stairs and railing.

13

Gatehouse and drawbridge

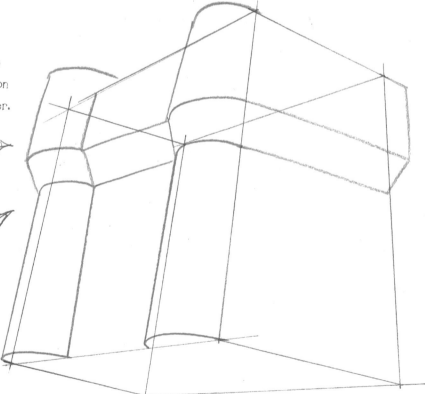

A drawbridge is usually over a moat or ditch and can be raised or lowered. At the first sign of danger the drawbridge would be raised, making it impossible for an enemy to cross into the castle.

Start by drawing a three-dimensional rectangular box shape using a vanishing point.

Give the gatehouse added drama by using a low eye level viewpoint.

Extend this section to make the upper section of the gatehouse larger.

Use curved lines to draw in the rounded sections of the gatehouse.

Add more detail.

Sketch in the battlements along the top of the walls.

Draw in the position of the door and windows.

Draw in the three-dimensional detail.

Complete the battlements by making them three-dimensional.

Softly draw in lines to create stonework.

Draw in wall and corner tower.

Finish by drawing the moat and adding a wooden drawbridge.

Add detail to the door and archway.

15

How castles developed

A castle is a fortress built for defence against enemy armies. It was also the home of a lord and his followers. People who lived on the castle lands were protected too.

Early castles consisted of a wooden tower built on an artificial mound or 'motte'.

A strong timber fence runs around the tower.

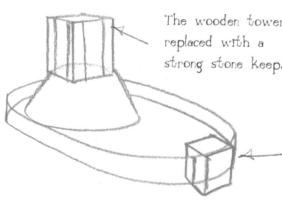

The wooden tower is replaced with a strong stone keep.

Add a box shape for the gatehouse.

The fenced enclosure is called a 'bailey'.

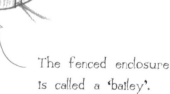

Draw in box shaped stone towers spaced along the 'curtain wall'.

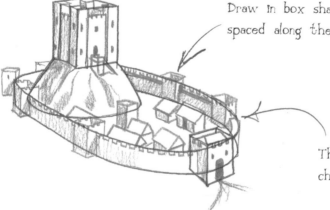

These outbuildings include a chapel and space for livestock.

Add details to the castle, gatehouse and battlements.

Draw in a rectangular box shape for the keep.

Draw in the outer walls with two rectangular shapes rounded off at the corners.

Add round watchtowers with pointed tops.

Draw in a more rectangular extra defending stone wall.

Sketch in rounded towers along both walls.

Add an archway.

Draw in flags.

A windmill was used to grind corn into flour.

Finish off all the windows and battlements.

Draw in a portcullis on both entrances.

Add a church spire, a windmill and lots of outbuildings.

Remove any unwanted construction lines.

17

Castle detail

Skilled archers could fire up to ten arrows a minute. A well-aimed arrow could kill a man almost a hundred metres away.

Castle walls often had battlements for defenders to hide behind.

Horizontal and vertical lines give the effect of stonework.

These holes in the floor were called 'murder holes'.

Use construction lines to help make the battlements look three-dimensional.

'Arrow loops' were often wider on the inside to give the archer a wider field of vision.

Use construction lines to help you experiment with proportion.

'Arrow loops' are the slits in the walls through which archers could fire arrows. These slits can be different shapes.

Bolts and handles can make a door look older and more realistic.

All the horizontal lines meet at the vanishing point.

19

Knights through the ages

Knights were not ordinary soldiers — they were the elite fighting men of their time. They travelled on horseback, wore high quality armour and used swords and lances.

Draw a simple stick figure.

Design your own shield markings.

Knights wore chainmail underneath their armour.

Sketch in nicks and dents on the shield to make it look more battleworn.

Add weapons to the knight's belt.

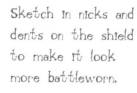

Shields and helmets came in different shapes and sizes.

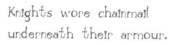

Draw simple stick figures to try out different stances or poses before you begin to draw.

Some helmets had visors to cover the knight's face.

The shield markings gave identity to each knight.

Knights wore armoured gloves (gauntlets).

Add shading to areas where light wouldn't reach.

Add spurs.

Add detail and shading to the metal armour. Leave some areas of the armour white as highlights on the metal surface.

Draw in a belt and chainmail skirt (jupon).

Remove any unwanted construction lines.

21

Knight

Knights were expected to be honourable and brave, and to protect the weak. This code of conduct became known as 'chivalry'.

Head

Draw a vertical line through the centre.

Main body

Draw in ovals for the head, neck, body and hips.

Hips

Centre line

Draw in the helmet.

Add circles for the hands.

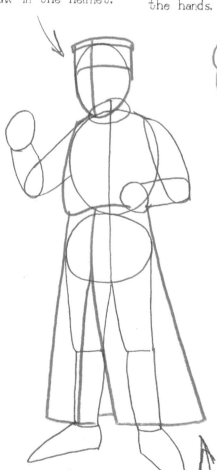

Light and shade
The shading in a drawing depends on the strength and direction of the light source. See how the shading is darker for all those parts of the knight's body furthest from the light source.

Draw in simple shapes for the feet.

Sketch in tube shapes for the arms and legs.

Use long sweeping lines for the knight's tunic.

Add more detail to the helmet.

Draw in the sword with the hand clenched around it.

Draw in the shield and strap.

Add vertical shading to the helmet to give the impression of metallic shine.

Sketch in the belt and scabbard.

Shade the sword.

Add chips and dents to the shield.

Turn the fabric back to create interest.

Draw a scale—like pattern for the chainmail.

Add a 'coat of arms' design to the shield and tunic.

Add the knee guards and spurs.

Add shading to the fabric to create soft folds.

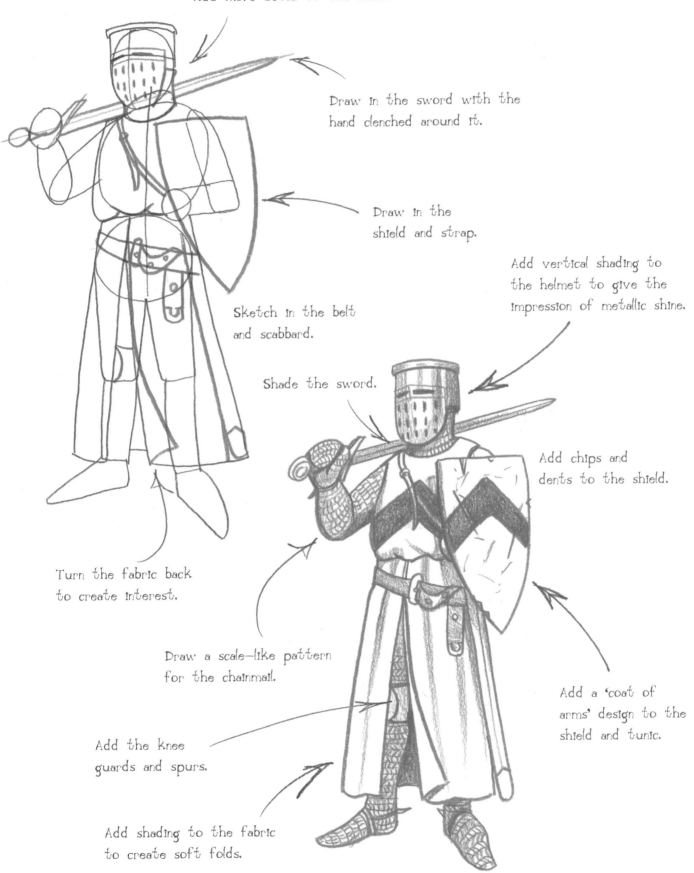

Remove any unwanted construction lines.

23

Knight on the attack

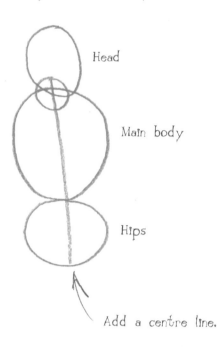

In times of war, a king would call up his knights and lords to fight. Battles were won by the knights and archers fighting together with a planned strategy of attack.

Draw three ovals for the head, neck, hips and main body.

Head

Main body

Hips

Add a centre line.

Draw a line to indicate the shoulders.

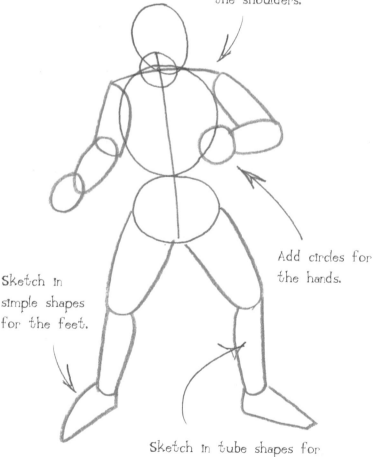

Add circles for the hands.

Sketch in simple shapes for the feet.

Sketch in tube shapes for the arms and legs.

Action poses

Try drawing basic stick figures to help you decide on a character's pose and how they might move.

Add a cone-shaped helmet and position the eyes, nose and mouth.

Draw a curved line around the face and across the chest for the chainmail hood.

Add a sword.

Sketch in the shield and strap.

Add a belt.

Draw in the gauntlets.

Draw in detail on the knight's armour, such as knee guards (poleyns).

Add the knight's foot guards (sabatons).

Finish drawing the face and helmet details.

Add a design to the knight's shield and tunic.

Shade in the sword.

Finish off all details on the knight's armour, belt and tunic.

Shade the areas where light wouldn't reach.

Add shade to the armour so it looks like metal.

Remove any unwanted construction lines.

25

Jousting Knight

In a joust, knights fought on a one—to—one basis. The knights charged at one another at great speed and tried to knock each other off their horses.

Draw in basic shapes for the knight's head, body and hips.

Add a curved line from the head, down the neck and across the back.

Knight body

Head

Front

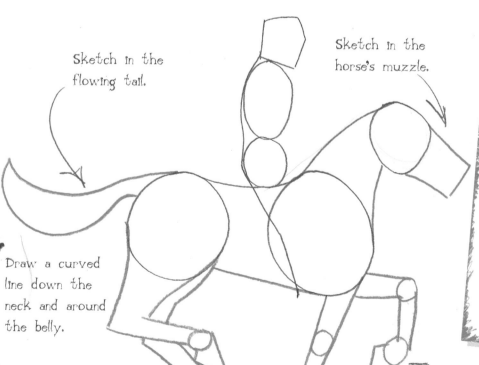

Hind quarters

Add a line for the knight's leg.

Draw a circular shape for the head and two larger ones for the body.

Sketch in the flowing tail.

Sketch in the horse's muzzle.

Draw a curved line down the neck and around the belly.

Using a mirror
Use a mirror to check out your drawing in reverse. This is a good way to spot mistakes.

Draw in the horse's legs and hooves. Add circles to indicate the joints.

Sketch in the decorative fabric on the helmet.

Use straight lines to draw in the lance.

Add a saddle and belt under the horse's belly.

Sketch in the horse's eyes, ears, mouth and nostrils. Indicate the horse's hood.

Add reins and stirrup.

Sketch in simple shapes for the knight's armour.

Use curved, flowing lines for the skirt of the horse's 'caparison' or 'surcoat'.

Add a crest and complete the detail of the helmet.

Add shield.

Use curved flowing lines for the horse's tail.

Add a dagger, shoulder guards and a belt.

Draw a 'coat of arms' design on to the horse's 'surcoat'.

Add tufts to the hooves.

Shade the areas where light would not reach.

Draw in a suggestion of the ground.

27

A travelling Knight

Knights setting off to fight in enemy territory had to take all kinds of supplies with them — clothes, food, weapons, armour, tents, bedding, medicines, spare horses and axes to cut firewood.

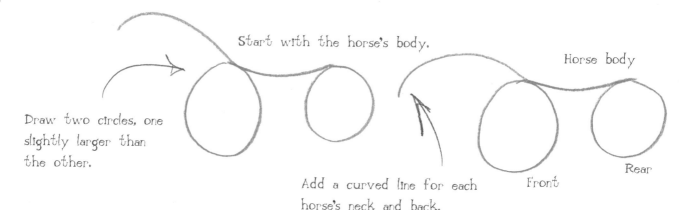

Start with the horse's body.

Draw two circles, one slightly larger than the other.

Add a curved line for each horse's neck and back.

Horse body

Front

Rear

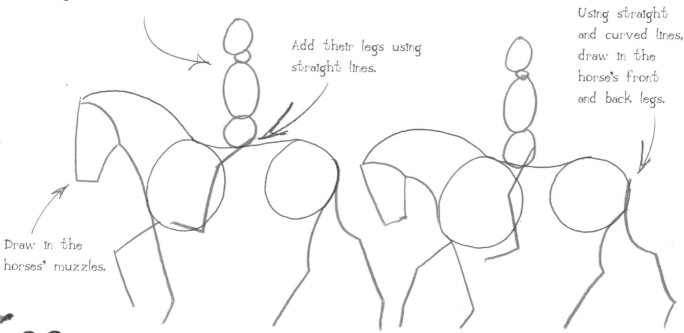

Draw simple shapes for the head, neck, body and hips of the knight and his steward.

Add their legs using straight lines.

Using straight and curved lines, draw in the horse's front and back legs.

Draw in the horses' muzzles.

Sketch in saddle and hand clutching a spear.

Add the knight's features, a helmet, armour and a shield.

Add the steward's features, headdress and clothing.

Draw in both horses' eyes and ears.

Draw in rounded shapes to indicate baggage.

Add reins, bridle and horse's mane.

Add the horses' tails

Draw in each horse's belly.

Draw in the horse's hooded surcoat and reins.

Sketch in both horses' legs and hooves.

Finish off the spear and add a flag.

Complete the steward's clothing.

Add detail to the knight's armour.

Draw the same 'coat of arms' on the shield and the horse's surcoat.

Shade the horses.

Add stirrups.

Shade in areas where the light doesn't reach.

29

Knights in battle

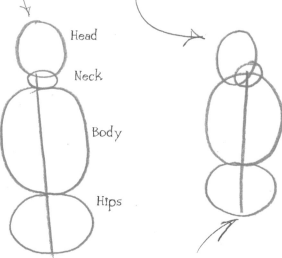

Knights fought with swords, lances, maces and battleaxes. This action pose shows two knights in battle, slashing at one another with their swords. It was vital that the sword blades were kept very sharp.

Draw in both figures using ovals for the head, neck, body and hips.

Head

Neck

Body

Hips

Add a vertical line to indicate the position of the body.

To show the right arm bent at the elbow, draw one oval smaller than the other and slightly overlapping.

Add the arms and legs using simple tube shapes.

Draw in circles for hands.

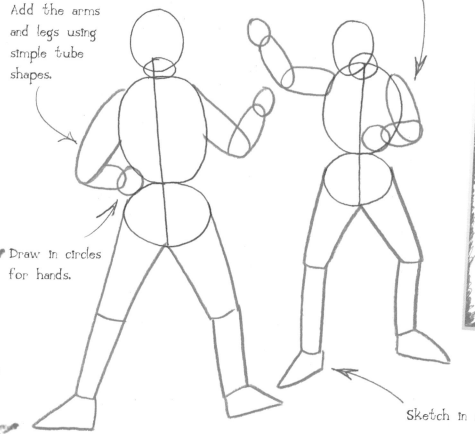

Composition

Framing your drawing in a square or a rectangle can make it look completely different.

Sketch in simple shapes for the feet.

30

Draw in the swords.

Sketch in fold lines on
the knight's back to
indicate movement.

Sketch in the eyes, nose and mouth.

Sketch different shaped helmets.

Draw in two shields.

Draw in the tunics.

Add shading to the
helmets to make
them look like metal.

Add shield markings and
nicked edges to create
a battleworn look.

Draw in a scaly pattern
for the knight's chainmail.

Draw in the
construction of
the back view
of this shield.

Add scabbards.

Add a battleground setting
with fallen helmets, shields
and fired arrows.

Add shadows to make the knights look three-dimensional.

31

Glossary

Centre line Often used as the starting point of the drawing, it marks the middle of the object or figure.

Composition The arrangement of the parts of a picture on the drawing paper.

Construction lines Guidelines used in the early stages of a drawing, and usually erased later.

Fixative A type of resin used to spray over a finished drawing to prevent smudging. **It should only be used by an adult.**

Light source The direction from which the light seems to come in a drawing.

Perspective A method of drawing in which near objects are shown larger than faraway objects to give an impression of depth.

Pose The position assumed by a figure.

Proportion The correct relationship of scale between each part of the drawing.

Silhouette A drawing that shows only a flat dark shape, like a shadow.

Vanishing point The place in a perspective drawing where parallel lines appear to meet.

Index